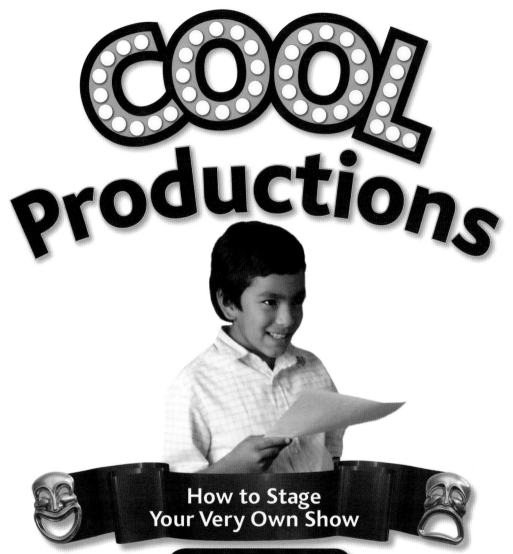

COOL
Productions

How to Stage Your Very Own Show

Karen Latchana Kenney

Consulting Editor, Diane Craig, M.A./Reading Specialist

ABDO
Publishing Company

Visit us at www.abdopublishing.com

Published by ABDO Publishing Company,
8000 West 78th Street, Edina, Minnesota 55439.
Copyright © 2010 by Abdo Consulting Group, Inc.
International copyrights reserved in all countries. No part
of this book may be reproduced in any form without written
permission from the publisher. The Checkerboard Library™
is a trademark and logo of ABDO Publishing Company.

Printed in the United States.
Design and Production: Colleen Dolphin, Mighty Media, Inc.
Photo Credits: Colleen Dolphin, Shutterstock,
iStockphoto (Zsolt Biczó, Pilar Echeverria, Michal Koziarski)
Series Editor: Katherine Hengel, Pam Price
Activity Production: Britney Haeg

The following manufacturers/names appearing in this book are
trademarks: Nestlé® Juicy Juice®, Office Depot® Posterboard

Library of Congress Cataloging-in-Publication Data

Kenney, Karen Latchana.
  Cool productions : how to stage your very own show / Karen
Latchana Kenney.
     p. cm. -- (Cool performances)
  Includes index.
  ISBN 978-1-60453-716-1
  1. Theater--Production and direction--Juvenile literature. I. Title.

PN2053.K375 2010
792.02'32--dc22
                              2009000405

Note to Adult Helpers

When it comes to putting on a show,
it is important for kids to have a little
help. Before beginning, find a good
place for kids to work. When children
are painting, make sure that they're
working in an approved space. Protect
surfaces with newspaper, an old sheet,
or cardboard.

If kids want to buy materials, ask them
to set a budget. Also remind them to
get permission from you before they
start painting, gluing, or cutting. Ask
them to clean up after themselves.
Finally, don't forget to encourage kids
as they put on their cool show!

Get the Picture!

There are many activities and how-to photos
in this title. Each how-to photo has a color
border around it, so match the border color
to the appropriate activity step!

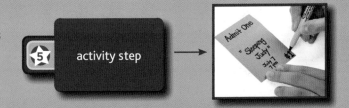

5 activity step

Contents

CREATING COOL PERFORMANCES

What's it all about?

Imagine putting on your very own show! Performing in front of an audience sounds fun, right? It is! You can pretend to be anything you want to be. Create an **illusion** through your costume, makeup, and stage. Tell a story by acting out a **script**. Put everything together, and you have a cool show!

You can create many kinds of shows. You can tell a funny story or a serious story. Put on a musical or a fairy tale. Creep out your audience with a monster or a ghost story. You can even be an alien on a strange planet!

Cool Performances Series

Cool Costumes	Cool Scripts & Acting
Cool Makeup	Cool Sets & Props
Cool Productions	Cool Special Effects

Permission

Before beginning, find out if you have permission to put on a show. To complete the activities in this book, you will be painting and hanging things. Ask an adult before you cut, paint, or hang anything.

Safety

- If you are using paint or glue, make sure you protect your work space so that it is not damaged.
- Wear work gloves and an old shirt when you are painting.
- Protect the floor with newspaper.
- If using a ladder, ask an adult to hold the bottom securely.

Clean Up

- Put away all tools and materials.
- Place lids on open containers.
- Throw away unusable scraps.
- Wipe down work surfaces.
- Store finished activities in an appropriate area.

Show Styles

There are many show styles. Shows can be one style or a combination of styles. Here are just a few.

Drama

Emotions are important in a drama. A dramatic show might be sad or it could make audiences laugh!

Fairy Tale

Fairy tales teach lessons. They have make-believe characters such as fairies, unicorns, and goblins.

Fantasy

Imaginary creatures make this kind of show fantastic! Mad scientists create monsters in laboratories, and aliens fly through space!

Musical

Singing is just as important as acting in a musical. Songs tell parts of the story.

THE BIG PERFORMANCE

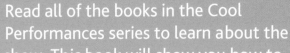

Putting the pieces together

The audience is seated, and the curtains slowly open. It's time for your big show! Putting on a show requires some planning, although you can plan a simple show in just an afternoon. Complicated shows can take a week or a month to plan. Decide what kind of show you want to do.

Read all of the books in the Cool Performances series to learn about the different parts of a show. This book will show you how to put all those parts together for your big performance.

First you will need a **script** and a stage. Get a **cast** together. Hold auditions or assign parts. Then it's time to rehearse. Before the performance, try a dress rehearsal with all the actors in costumes and makeup. Make sure your stage is set up and your special effects are in place. This is a great way to see how everything comes together.

If you want an audience, you need to advertise your show. Get the word out with posters and flyers. **Cast** members can give them to friends and family members. You can also make programs, tickets, and a banner for your show.

Finally, after all of your planning and work, it's time for the first big performance. This is called opening night. Get your audience warmed up before the show begins. Tell some jokes while the actors get into their spots on stage. You might want to have an intermission during the show. Intermission is a break when treats and drinks are served. It is also a great time to rearrange the stage. At the end of the performance, get ready to take a bow.

One last thing: don't forget about the strike and cast party! Striking the set is when you take down the scenery and clean up the stage. The cast party is your time to relax. Talk about how fun the performance was and congratulate yourselves. What a great show!

BEHIND THE SCENES

Every show needs a **cast** to act out the **script**. But the people behind the scenes are just as important as the actors! These people are in charge of the different parts of a show. Together, they are called the **production** team. Here are their titles and roles in a production.

Costume designers create costumes for professional shows. If the story is set in the past, they research the clothing from that time to create the costumes. Or, they might make unique costumes for fantasy characters. Costume designers study the script and work with the director to make sure the costumes are right for the show.

Lighting designers decide where to place the lights and when to use them in a production. A **cue sheet** can help the designers remember when to use specific types of light.

Set designers focus on the stage's background. They create the sets in professional shows. They study the script and decide how the stage should look. They also work with the director to make sure the set matches what the director has in mind.

Makeup designers apply makeup to actors. They study ways to make different looks. They can create a woman from the 1960s or a lion's face for a Broadway musical. They use brushes and **applicators** to apply theatrical makeup. Theatrical makeup has vibrant colors and won't melt under the bright lights and heat on stage.

Musical directors are in charge of the music in the show. They instruct the musicians and decide which **cast** members will sing the songs. A musical director might also pick prerecorded songs to play during a show.

Sound designers study **scripts** and decide how to add to the story with sound effects. Car horns and howling winds are examples of sound effects. Sound effects can be prerecorded and played during a show, or they can be created during the actual show. A sound designer also sets up the microphones and sound systems for big **productions**.

Special effects technicians are specially trained to design effects and run effects machines. Big productions sometimes create dangerous effects such as thunder and lightning or smoke and fire. That is why these trained technicians are so important. They protect the actors and the audience.

A LOOK AT A THEATER

The fly space is by the ceiling and is usually covered with a short curtain. It hides rolled-up **backdrops**.

Curtains separate the stage from the audience.

Wings are the sides of the stage where actors can make their entrances and exits.

The deck is the floor of the stage. It is separated into different areas called stage directions.

The house is where the audience sits in a theater.

fly space

curtains

wings

deck

house

SHOW TIMELINES

Whether you have a day, a week, or a month to create your show, it helps to have a timeline. Study the following timeline samples, and then make your own!

In a Day

9 A.M. – 10 A.M.
Find some friends to be in the cast. Write a short script. Make sure there are enough parts for your cast.

10 A.M. – NOON
Make your set. Find things at home to use. Build anything else you need. Or, just paint a cool backdrop.

NOON – 12:30 P.M.
Take a lunch break. You'll need energy to put on your show!

12:30 P.M. – 1:00 P.M.
Find a good stage for your show.

1:00 P.M. – 2:00 P.M.
Make your costumes. Keep them simple. Old hats and scarves might work.

2:00 P.M. – 3:00 P.M.
Rehearse your show on the stage. Try going through it a couple of times.

3:00 P.M. – 4:00 P.M.
Set up your stage. Hang up the backdrop. Move in your set pieces.

4:00 P.M. – 5:00 P.M.
Get ready for the show. Put on your costumes.

5:00 P.M.
It's showtime!

In a Week

Day 1
- See who wants to put on a show.
- Find a script to use. Or write one based on your favorite story.
- Pick your stage area.
- Make a list of the costumes, set pieces, props, special effects, and makeup that you want to use in the show. See what you already have. Make a list of what you still need.

Day 2
- Set a budget and decide what you can buy.
- Ask an adult to take you shopping for your supplies. Go to dollar and thrift stores.
- Look in the newspaper for garage sales.

Day 3
- Make a poster for your show. Put it up for friends and family to see.
- Invite your friends over to create the set pieces and props.

Day 4
- Put together the costumes for the show. Have your friends help. They should try on their costumes as well.

Day 5
- This is the day for the cast to learn their lines. Have cast members study the script at home.
- Try putting on your stage makeup.
- Practice so you will get it right.

Day 6
- Time to rehearse! Get the cast together. At the beginning of the day, just practice your lines together. At the end of the day, try a dress rehearsal on your stage.
- Set up your stage. Hang the backdrop.
- Put out your set pieces and props. Get your special effects materials ready. Make sure your lighting works.

Day 7
- Ask everyone to meet an hour before the show.
- Set up a concession stand if you have an intermission.
- Get into costume and apply makeup. Then get ready to perform.
- It's showtime!

13

In a Month

Week 1

- Set your budget for the show.
- Find a script to use or write one.
- Look for a performance and rehearsal space. See if you can use the stage at your school or community center!
- Pick a date for the performance.
- Decide which set pieces, props, and costumes you will need for the show.
- Make a list of the supplies you will need. Figure out what you will need for special effects. Decide what makeup you need to buy.

14

Week 2

- Put your cast together. Hold auditions or pick friends who want to be in the show.
- Give each cast member a copy of the script. Ask them to study their lines.
- Buy the supplies needed to make set pieces, props, special effects, costumes, and promotional materials. Buy stage makeup as well.
- Make all of the promotional materials.
- Create a poster. Make flyers and give them to cast members to hand out. Paint a banner and make tickets.
- Build set pieces and make props. Get cast members to help.

Week 3

- Start rehearsals. Gather at the rehearsal space every day and run through the show.
- Begin making the costumes for the show. Have cast members help.
- Practice putting on stage makeup.

Week 4

- Hold dress rehearsals.
- Rehearse the special effects you will use.
- Make sure the costumes fit the cast members.
- Get ready for opening night! Ask the cast to show up an hour early to get into costume and apply makeup. Set up the concession stand and the theater.

STAGE KIT

banner paper

poster board

To comp
the activi
this boo
will need
basic ma

tempera paint

markers

paintbrushes

scissors

masking tape

colored pencils

pencil

ruler

beverages

perforating tool

cutting mat

tablecloth

work gloves

old shirt

napkins

paper

small table

snacks

Poster Promotion

Get the word out! Create some **buzz** about your show! Use posters, banners, and flyers to tell people about your **production**. These efforts are called advertising. The more people who know about your show, the bigger your audience will be.

STAGE KIT

- poster board
- markers or colored pencils
- masking tape

Sleeping Judy
Saturday, July 7
7 pm
in Lisa's Living Room
Adm: $1
The Encore Entourage

Get a group of friends together and get creative! Decide on a main image for your show such as:
- a UFO or a rocket ship for a show about aliens or space travel
- a castle for a fairy tale
- ghosts or a haunted house for a scary show

Take Two!

You can create ads for your show on a computer. Use a graphics or a word-processing program to make flyers, brochures, and banners. For fun, add photographs of **cast** members in costume!

Give each person a piece of poster board. Use markers or colored pencils. Have each person draw a rectangular box at the top or bottom of the poster. In this box, write the following information in big letters:
- title of the show
- date and time of the show
- where the show will be
- admission price (if you are selling tickets)
- name of the group putting on the show

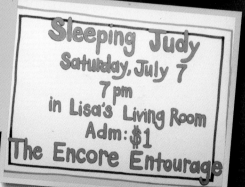

Sleeping Judy
Saturday, July 7
7 pm
in Lisa's Living Room
Adm: $1
The Encore Entourage

Put your posters up using masking tape. Get permission from an adult first. If you are inviting people from your community, see if you can put up posters in your school or community center. If you are only inviting your families, ask family members to put posters up in their homes.

Fun Flyers

STAGE KIT

- paper,
8.5 x 11 inches
(21.6 x 27.9 cm)
- markers

The Encore Entourage presents:

Sleeping Judy

a magical modern-day fairy tale!

Sat. July 7
7 pm
Lisa's Living $1

1 Write all of the information from your poster (see pages 18 and 19) on a piece of paper.

2 Go to a copy shop and make some copies. Make color copies or copy the flyer on colored paper.

3 Hand out the flyers to neighbors or other kids you want to invite to your show. Ask for an adult's permission first though!

Cool Banner

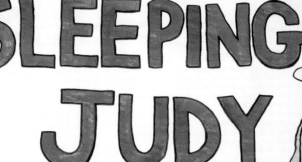

SLEEPING JUDY

SATURDAY, JULY 7
7 pm

 1 Using a pencil, sketch a design on the banner paper. Write the title of your show in big letters. Next, write in the date and time of the performance.

 3 Paint your banner with bright colors. Make sure there is fresh air in your work space. Wear work gloves and an old shirt.

 2 Draw a few cool pictures that say something about your show.

 4 When your banner is dry, use a black marker to outline the words. Then use masking tape to hang your banner near your stage.

Tear-Off Tickets

Make your production an official success! Create your own tickets that you can give (or sell!) to your audience members.

Admit One

STAGE KIT

- paper, 8.5 x 11 inches (21.6 x 27.9 cm)
- scissors
- cutting mat
- ruler
- pencil
- perforating tool
- markers

" Sleeping Judy "

July 7
7 pm

$1

1. Fold a piece of paper in half 3 times so that you have eight rectangles as shown. Each rectangle will be a ticket. Use more than one piece of paper if needed. Cut out your tickets.

2. Place a ticket on the cutting mat with the long side of the ticket at the top as shown. Use a ruler and pencil to make a small mark that is 2.75 inches (7 cm) from the left side of the ticket. Draw a **faint** vertical line over your mark. Run the perforating tool over the line.

3. Using markers, write the name of the show on the large part of the ticket. Then, write *Admit One* on the small part of the ticket.

4. Tear off the smaller part of the ticket as people enter your show. Encourage them to keep the big part of the ticket as a souvenir!

The Program

Guide your audience through your show with a program! It lists the actors, the **production** team, and the show schedule.

The Encore Entourage Presents:

Sleeping Judy

1 Fold a piece of paper so the short ends meet. Position it like a book, with the open edge on the right side. Now draw a cool cover that includes the title of your show.

2 Open up the program. On the left-hand side, make a list of the characters and the actors who perform the roles. Title this section *Characters*. Below the character list, add the **production** team. Include anyone who helped put on the show. Title this section *Crew*.

3 On the right-hand side, write the title at the top of the page. Below that, write the show schedule. If the show has different acts, list and describe each one. Will there be an intermission? Tell the audience how long it will last and whether or not there will be snacks and drinks.

4 On the back of the program, thank everyone who helped you put on your show. Include the owners of the performance space and the people who donated things for you to use. This could be your parents, brothers, or sisters! Repeat these steps to make more programs. Or make copies at a copy shop.

Intermission Treats

It's fun to enjoy beverages and treats when you watch a show! It's just like when you go to movies! Set out some of your favorite snacks for your audience to enjoy.

STAGE KIT
- small table
- tablecloth
- poster board
- markers
- masking tape
- snacks
- beverages
- price list and money to make change (opt.)
- napkins

Theater Treats

Put a small table at the back of the theater. Place a tablecloth over the table. This will be your concession stand.

Decide what kinds of snacks and beverages you would like to serve during intermission. For example, you could serve cookies, popcorn, juice boxes and water.

Use poster board and markers to make a sign for the stand. Write *Concession Stand* in big letters. Or make up a fun name such as *Theater Treats* or *Super Snacks*.

If you are charging a fee for snacks and beverages, make a sign that shows the price for each item. Have some dollar bills and change ready.

Price List
Theater Treats

Popcorn.........25¢

cookies........50¢

bottled $1.00
Water

juice .... 75¢

On the day of the big performance, set out your snacks, beverages, and napkins just before the intermission begins!

Strike It!

After the show, you need to clean up the stage and the theater. Remember to:

- Fold up costumes and store them in a box. Or hang them in a storage closet.

- Put the props and set pieces in storage. Throw away or donate anything you do not want to keep.

- Gather all the chairs and put them back where they belong.

- Sweep the stage and the audience area.

- Take down all of the banners, signs, and posters.

- Put trash and recyclables in the proper bins and containers.

Cast Party!

After all of your hard work, it's time to celebrate!

Have a party for everyone involved in the show. A **cast** party is a great way to relax. Talk about how the show went. Eat some cookies and laugh about any mistakes that happened. Invite audience members to join you. Ask for their opinions. Sit back, relax, and think about the next show that you want to create!

CONCLUSION

Bravo! Take a bow. Your show is finished! It is a lot of work to put on a show, but it's worth it. Wasn't it fun to see your audience having such a great time? Did you enjoy their applause?

Cool Productions is about making your show a reality. Check out the other books in the Cool Performances series to learn more about putting on a show. Learn how to use makeup and costumes to create different looks. Practice your acting skills and try writing a **script**. Add lighting and special effects. Create unique sets and props. Have fun and let your imagination run wild!

GLOSSARY

applicator – a device used to apply something.

backdrop – a painted cloth or banner hung across the back of a stage.

buzz – excitement or attention about something new or an upcoming event.

cast – 1) a group of actors who perform together. 2) to give an actor a role in a performance.

cue sheet – a document that contains hints or signals for performers.

faint – not totally clear.

illusion – something that seems real but isn't.

production – the act or process of making something.

script – the written text for a performance.

Web Sites

To learn more about putting on a show, visit ABDO Publishing Company on the World Wide Web at www.abdopublishing.com. Web sites about theater are featured on our Book Links page. These links are routinely monitored and updated to provide the most current information available.

INDEX